nigel risner

To Jack

It's a zoo around here!

The new rules for better communication

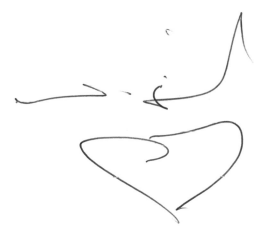

Limitless Publications

Third Edition published in 2005 by
Limitless Publications
Garden House
Garden Close
Arkley Herts EN5 3EW
England

Printed in Great Britain by
Philtone Printing Ltd
Bristol

Graphic Design by
Joanne Bloomfield
e-mail: joanne@bsolutions.co.uk
www.bsolutions.co.uk

ISBN 0-9546836-0-9

Acknowledgments

I would like to thank my clients for their responses to this material as it has been presented in workshops and seminars. Their feed-back has helped me to refine the basic concepts and develop practical applications that really work.

My everlasting gratitude to Fran, my wife, who has let me out of my cage to be the person I need to be, as ever you are my rock.

Daniel & Sasha, my two amazing kids who are a constant joy.

Mum & Dad for keeping my feet firmly on the ground.

Ali my PA. who keeps me on the road to do my stuff.

Joanne Bloomfield for transforming the presentation and quality of my marketing material and books.

If you go to the zoo,
always take something to
feed the animals......even
if the sign says
"Do not feed the animals"
It wasn't the animals that
put them signs up.

from The Wit and Wisdom of Forrest Gump

Contents

What's all this about animals?

You won't like this book. You'll probably hate it. In fact, at this very moment you're probably thinking: "Oh no. Not another writer who wants to squeeze people into cages!"

But I guarantee that if you read it, it will change your life.

This book will give you a whole new perspective on people and relationships, and you will never be the same again.

The idea behind it is that although we are all individuals, we do have common personality traits that affect the way we communicate. As we learn to recognise the different communication styles that work best for different people and different situations, we can become more effective communicators in every aspect of our lives.

I like to think of people as either monkeys, lions, dolphins or elephants, depending on the communication style they use most often. Anyone who needs to communicate with a variety of people can think of themselves as a zoo keeper who wants to understand what makes the various animals tick.

I speak to about 150 audiences per year. It's relatively easy to identify how some of them communicate. For example, The Academy for Chief Executives and TEC International tend to be made up of lions. The Samaritans and The Body Shop employ dolphins. The people working for Red Bull and The Institute of Sales and Marketing are monkeys, while Deloitte & Touche and The Royal Institute of Chartered Surveyors have plenty of elephants.

But often you have to talk to groups that include people with the full spectrum of communication styles. How do you know who's who? Nobody holds up a sign saying "I'm a monkey" or "I'm a lion". And how do you talk to people whose style is different from yours?

Remember Dr Dolittle? He was able to talk to all the animals and hear what they were telling him. Wouldn't it be great if we could do the same! My aim in this book is to help you take steps in that direction.

My focus here is not on labelling people, but rather on understanding them better and having more fun together at work and at home.

One of my favourite sayings is "If you're in the room, be in the room!" And how important that is when were trying to relate to and communicate with other people. If you find you're having trouble communicating with someone, chances are you're not really paying attention.

Our lives are so busy it's easy to fall into the trap of trying to concentrate on more than one thing at a time - deadly if you're trying to relate to another person. So if you're in the room, be in the room, and you'll find your communication skills sky-rocket!

The point of my approach is that if we can recognise the needs different people have, and identify their communication styles, we can adapt our own style and so communicate better. Believe me, to do that effectively you really need to be in the room!

Nigel's simple animal matrix
for identifying personality traits

Lion	Monkey
(Orange Pages)	(Yellow Pages)
Single - minded	Playful
Visionary	Energetic
Straight forward	Extrovert
Purposeful	Lively
Persevering	Persuasive
Elephant	**Dolphin**
(Green Pages)	(Blue Pages)
Cautious	Caring
Meticulous	Nurturing
Deliberate	Supportive
Skeptical	Patient
Formal	Relaxed

How to approach this book

How you read this book is entirely up to you. If you'd like to start with the section that describes your own communication style, the questions below will point you in the right direction.

- Do you like excitement, action and inspiration?
- Are you easily bored by facts, figures and detailed analysis?
- Do you enjoy being with people who know how to have fun?

  If so, turn to the yellow section of the book.

- Are you ambitious and independent?
- Do you like taking the initiative, organising people and getting things done?
- Would other people describe you as self-confident?

  If so, the orange section is for you.

- Are you friendly and understanding?
- Do you try to reduce conflict between people?
- Is it difficult for you to say no when someone asks you to help?

  If so, why not dive right into the blue section?

- Are you good at studying and solving problems?
- Do ideas fascinate you?
- Before reaching a decision, do you like to gather as many facts and opinions as possible?

  If so, go straight to the green section.

If the questions above don't suggest a category that fits you, don't give up. Think for a moment about your personal preferences and look for general trends in your communication style. This will probably narrow the field down a bit.

I find that 95% of people have one clearly dominant trait, and this may be where you want to start. You could begin by reading the section that represents the larger part of you, and then move on to the next one.

Alternatively, you may prefer to read the book right through in the usual way. The material has been designed to suit individual reader's interests, so dipping and skipping will work just as well as reading from cover to cover. For example, you may have colleagues whose communication styles differ hugely from yours. After reading the section that relates most closely to you, why not read about their styles in turn?

Whichever way you choose to approach the book, I hope you'll stay with me and read it all eventually. My objective is to help readers understand themselves and other people better so that all their relationships improve. The more we understand where people (including ourselves) are coming from, the better we can relate to each other. As a result, communication becomes more satisfying and everybody benefits.

You will also note that I have left plenty of space in the key sections of the book. Make notes about yourself, your family and your colleagues. The more you interact with the book, the more beneficial it will be.

For Elephants only

People often ask, "How can billions of people fall into only four types?"

Good question. But remember, people fall into only three or four races: Negroid, Mongolian/Caucasian, and Indian.

Of course we are all unique individuals, with our own likes, dislikes, talents and passions - and no classifying system can do justice to that! What a system can do, though, is identify tendencies and patterns across large groups of people.

Any kind of analysis of communication styles is going to be complex because there are so many variables affecting the way we relate to each other. In the 1980s and 1990s some psychologists (e.g. Krahé and Hampson) suggested that our judgements of someone else's personality can never be neutral or objective because our own assumptions will come into play. Those ssumptions will influence the way we interpret the other person.

Nevertheless, categories are extremely useful in helping us make sense of our world.

Most readers will recognise aspects of themselves in more than one of the categories I've outlined here, especially as different situations and contexts influence their behaviour. It's very unusual to find a person who fits into all four categories, though many people have secondary traits that enable them to straddle two or three categories.

If you would like to read about personality and communication styles in more detail, the following systems may interest you:

- Belbin
- DISC
- Myers-Briggs
- Carl Jung

To find what you need, surf the net or browse in your local library. If you want to explore gender differences in communication styles, there's a great book by Barbara and Allan Pease called **Why Men Don't Listen and Women Can't Read Maps.**

I recommend it.

Clients who have found this system useful include:

ACE	Lloyds TSB
BAA	Marks and Spencer
Barclays	Mars
Body Shop	Pepsi/7-UP
BP	Pfizer
Compaq	Red Bull
Debenhams	Royal Bank of Scotland
Exel	Siemens
Gartmore Investments	TEC
HSBC	Zurich Life Assurance

If you think that you are
too small to have an impact
try going to bed with a
mosquito in the room.

Author unknown

The zoo keeper's challenge

You shouldn't try to
teach a pig to sing.
It's a waste of your time
and it annoys the pig.

Mark Twain

The zoo keeper's challenge

For the purposes of this book, a zoo keeper could be anyone who works with a variety of people and wants to understand them better.

Zoo keepers each have their own communication style as well. The more they understand themselves, the better they can relate to other people.

Being an effective zoo keeper means knowing each of the animals in your care, understanding what makes them tick, putting them in the best possible surroundings and feeding them the right kind of food.

The most effective teams are made up of people who are different from each other but have learned to work together creatively. As a zoo keeper, your task is to facilitate that process wherever you can. This includes helping individuals to find the best niche for their particular talents and skills.

A mother camel and her baby were lazing around in the sun. Suddenly the baby said, "Mother, Mother, can I ask you something?"

"Sure," said the mother. "Is something bothering you, Son?"

"Why do camels have humps?" he asked.

"Well, Son, we are desert animals. We need the humps to store water so that we can survive where there is no water to drink."

"OK," said the baby, "then why are our legs long and our feet rounded?"

"Son, obviously they are meant for walking in the desert. You know, with these legs I can move around the desert better than anyone."

"OK, then why are our eye lashes so long? Sometimes they bother my sight."

"My Son, those long, thick eye lashes are your protective cover. They help to protect your eyes from the desert sand and wind," said the mother, her eyes brimming with pride.

"I see," said the baby. "So the hump is to store water when we are in the desert, the legs are for walking through the desert and these eye lashes protect our eyes from the desert. Then what the hell are we doing here in a zoo?"

Skills, knowledge, abilities and experience are only useful if the right person is in the right place at the right time. Facilitating that is part of your challenge as a zoo keeper.

Over the centuries there have been many people who have described personality traits as a means of classifying people.

In the 5th century BC, Hippocrates described four humours: choleric, melancholic, phlegmatic and sanguine.

More recently Carl Jung described four functions (thinking, intuition, feeling and sensation) and four attitudes (extrovert, judgmental, introvert and perceptive). These types later formed the basis of the 16 Myers-Briggs codes: ENTP, ENTJ, ENFJ, INTJ, INFP, INFJ, ESFP, ESFJ, ESTP, ESTJ, INTP, ISTJ, ISFP, ISFJ, ENFP and ISTP.

Friedman worked with chemical types to describe people as either Type A or Type B. And in Sperry's typology of different brain functions, people can be described as favouring either the left side or the right side of their brain.

Turner and Greco describe a Personality Compass which comprises four categories:

- North (motto: gets the job done fast)

- East (motto: does it right the first time)

- South (motto: builds the best teams)

- West (motto: expands all horizons)

13

My system also works with four types. It focuses on people's dominant communication styles and links each one with a particular animal, just for fun:

- the monkey

- the lion

- the dolphin

- the elephant

To be an effective zoo keeper, you need to understand each style - your own, and those of the people with whom you work. This will give you a greater insight into the individuals who make up your team. As you recognise what makes each person special and find ways to tap into the groups diversity, your team will grow stronger. When individuals are encouraged to work to their strengths, it brings out the best in everyone.

But it's hard work, and you won't like everything you discover. So fasten your seat belt and get ready to be taken a long, long way from your comfort zone.

Know your animals

One of your most valuable skills as a zoo keeper is your ability to understand your animals. They are constantly sending you signals about their needs and feelings. When you can interpret these correctly you'll know how to work with them most effectively. So what is there to know?

Human animals have many subtle ways of communicating. You can pick up their signals if all your senses are tuned in. When you are aware of the visual, aural, kinesthetic, emotional, and other sensory cues that they are transmitting, you will know how to relate to them. You'll know when up or slow down, when to focus on the details, or when to work on building your relationship with the other person.

We all have the same basic human needs, but you may measure success differently from the way I do.

Some people measure success by results. They'll work their hearts out to get the job done. They are prepared to sacrifice a great deal to achieve the finished product because that's how they measure success. They need to accomplish something tangible.

Other people measure success in terms of their relationships. These individuals are typically sensitive, warm and supportive. They will work well if they feel that they and their colleagues are valued. They put people before results.

Then there are those who measure their success in terms of the recognition they receive. They need to know that others think highly of them and their work. Acknowledgement and praise are very important to them.

Finally there are the people who are more concerned with the content than the congratulations. They like things to be well structured and organised and clearly understood. They measure success by the quality of the work they produce. Usually they are able to measure the quality themselves - they don't need anyone else to tell them when they've done a good job.

The skillful zoo keeper recognises that each of these four types will respond to different strategies. Once you realise this you can work out how best to communicate with a wide variety of people.

Managers who understand the different needs of the people in their team can find ways to appeal to the best in each individual. This principle holds true for anyone who wants to relate more effectively to other people. Families benefit from this as much as any other team. Sometimes we make the mistake of thinking that the members of our family are more like clones than individuals. Good zoo keeping begins at home!

The good zoo keeper is observant, always looking for clues that will help to explain why people behave the way they do. It's important to tune into body language as well as what is said and not said. One useful way of identifying a person's communication style is by noticing two dimensions: openness and directness.

People whose style is open are relaxed, informal, personable, responsive and warm. They express their feelings freely, and place a high value on relationships. Open people are happy to talk about themselves and their families, and to share personal stories.

The good zoo keeper will notice that open people are flexible about time. When making decisions they tend to trust their intuition and opinion more than the facts. They tend to be flamboyant characters and their body language will show you how they are feeling.

At the other end of the openness spectrum are the guarded individuals. These people come across as reserved, formal and aloof. Guarded people keep their private lives to themselves.

The good zoo keeper will observe that guarded people tend to follow the rules. They are very time-conscious and disciplined. Their decisions will be based on facts, and they are unlikely to be swayed by popular opinion.

The second dimension is directness. This indicates how far a person tries to control situations or other people.

Direct people like taking initiatives and being active. They tend to be quick, decisive, and willing to take risks. They come across as confident, even dominant at times, and have trouble being patient with people who are slower-paced. Direct people talk and express opinions freely and emphatically.

Indirect people appear to be more thoughtful and to operate at a more measured pace. They avoid risks, preferring to ask questions and gather information before making a decision. Indirect people tend to be quiet and reserved, and listen rather than talk. They come across as supportive and relaxed.

Openness and directness levels vary from person to person. An individual may be high in one and low in the other, or somewhere in between.

When directness is combined with openness it forms four different, recognisable, and habitual behavioural styles: the socialiser, the director, the thinker, and the relater. The name given to each style reflects a very general characteristic rather than a full or accurate description.

As you develop your understanding of why people behave the way they do, your ability to communicate with them will increase, and they will feel more comfortable interacting with you.

Monkey; Open and Direct

The monkey has high levels of both directness and openness. Monkeys are animated, intuitive, lively. They are ideas people, and can get very enthusiastic about their plans. However, others may see them as manipulative.

Monkeys are fast-paced people who act and make decisions spontaneously. They are not concerned about facts and details, and try to avoid them as much as possible. This disregard for details may prompt them at times to exaggerate and generalise facts and figures.

Monkeys are more comfortable with "best guesstimates" than with carefully researched facts. They thrive on involvement with people and usually work quickly and enthusiastically with others.

Monkeys always seem to be chasing dreams. They are so persuasive that others can easily get caught up in their dreams. Monkeys always seem to be seeking approval and pats on the back for their accomplishments and achievements. They are socialisers: creative, dynamic and able to think on their feet.

Lion: direct and guarded

Lions are very direct and at the same time guarded. They exhibit firmness in their relationships with others, are oriented toward productivity and goals, and are concerned with bottom-line results. Closely allied to these positive traits, however, are some negative ones: the lion can be stubborn, impatient, tough and even domineering.

Lions tend to take control of other people and situations and be decisive in both their actions and decisions. They like to move at an extremely fast pace and are very impatient with delays. When other people can' t keep up with their speed, they view them as incompetent. The lion' s motto might well be " I want it done right and l want it done now."

Lions are typically high achievers who exhibit very good administrative skills; they certainly get things done and make things happen.

Lions like to do many things at the same time. They may start by juggling three things at the same time, and as soon as they feel comfortable with those they pick up a fourth. They keep adding on until the pressure builds to such a point that they turn their backs and let everything drop. Then they turn right around and start the whole process all over again.

Elephant: indirect and guarded

People who have the elephant behaviour are both indirect and guarded. They seem to be very concerned with the process of thinking, and are persistent, systematic problem-solvers. But they also can be seen as aloof, picky and critical. Elephants are very security-conscious and have a strong need to be right. This leads them to an over-reliance on data collection. In their quest for data they tend to ask lots of questions about specific details. This can be infuriating to monkeys and lions.

Elephants actions and decisions tend to be extremely cautious. They tend to work slowly and precisely by themselves and prefer an intellectual work environment that is organised and structured. They tend to be sceptical and like to see things in writing.

Although they are great problem-solvers, elephants are poor decision-makers. They may keep collecting data even beyond the time when a decision is due, justifying their caution by saying, "When you are making vast decisions, you cannot do it on half-vast data."

Dolphin: open and indirect

The fourth and last style, the dolphin, is open and unassertive, warm, supportive, and reliable. However, the dolphin sometimes is seen by others as compliant, soft-hearted, and acquiescent. Dolphins seek security and like to feel they belong. Like the elephant, the dolphin is slow at taking action and making decisions. This procrastination stems from a desire to avoid risky and unknown situations. Before dolphins take action or make decisions, they have to know how other people feel.

The dolphin is the most people-oriented of all four styles. Having close, friendly, personal, and first-name relationships with others is one of the most important objectives of the dolphin's style.

Dolphins dislike interpersonal conflicts so much that they sometimes say what they think other people want to hear rather than what they really think. Dolphins have tremendous counselling skills and are extremely supportive of other people. They are also incredibly active listeners. You usually feel good just being with a relater. Because dolphins listen so well to other people, when it is their turn to talk, people usually listen. This gives them an excellent ability to gain support from others.

Look, I really don't want to wax philosophical, but I will say that if you're alive, you got to flap your arms and legs, you got to jump around a lot, you got to make a lot of noise, because life is the very opposite of death. And therefore, as I see it, if you're quiet, you're not living. You've got to be noisy, or at least your thoughts should be noisy and colourful and lively.

Mel Brooks

I saw a young mother
With eyes full of laughter
And two little shadows
Came following after.

Wherever she moved,
They were always right there
Holding onto her skirts,
Hanging onto her chair.
Before her, behind her -
An adhesive pair.

"Don't you ever get weary
As, day after day,
Your two little tagalongs
Get in your way?"

She smiled as she shook
Her pretty young head,
And I'll always remember
The words that she said:

"It's good to have shadows
That run when you run,
That laugh when you're happy
And hum when you hum -
For you only have shadows
When your life's filled with sun."

Author unknown

24

Dominant characteristics of the monkey

Has plenty of ideas

Knows how to have fun

Enjoys a joke

Is very creative

Likes examples and pictures

Gets bored easily

Other people may see the monkey as

A charlatan

Noisy

Manipulative

Not serious

Unreliable

Aggressive

An exhibitionist

Creative

Dynamic

Friendly

Imaginative

How to address monkeys

Ask them for ideas.

Be energetic.

Make it fun.

Appointments and punctuality

Monkeys prefer others to be punctual but this isn't crucial. If you're late, it's probably OK.

They often arrive late themselves but can learn and adapt.

To initiate a conversation with a monkey

Keep greetings short.

Always include a little story or joke.

Conversational structure

Be enthusiastic.

Inspire them.

Focus on their ideas.

Tap into their creativity.

How to change a monkey's way of thinking and operating

You can't: only they can.

Monkeys could say one thing and then say another later and mean both.

How to present change

Monkeys need space.

They need to be included but may not know how to achieve the change.

Tap into their ideas.

What about mistakes?

Instead of telling monkeys about any mistakes that have been made, ask them to find out what happened. They will often be more creative than other people.

Communicating negative feedback

Talk to the monkey in private.

Be prepared to argue.

Use the "sandwich" technique as a cushioning device:

* Build them up (the first banana)

* Give them the feedback (the nut)

* Build them up again (the second banana)

What do monkeys hate most?

Authority (and hearing that they must or have to do something)

Details

Reports

How do monkeys express anger?

They may step on your toes.

They'll probably explode and then get over it, pick up the pieces and apologise.

How to acknowledge a monkey

Heap on the praise.

There's no limit to the monkey's love of recognition.

If doing this by e-mail, cc it to the rest of the world!

Getting monkeys to co-operate

Excite them.

Fuel their enthusiasm.

Monkeys want to show you that you need them.

Ask them for help.

Additional issues

Monkeys hate long-term missions.

Agendas and Powerpoint presentations don't mean much to them.

Pictures give them greater clarity than abstractions do.

Monkeys want to play, even to their own detriment. If something more interesting comes up, they'll want to do that regardless of prior agreements. So make sure they're clear about what needs to be done, and they're committed to it.

People who laugh actually
live longer than those who
don't laugh. Few persons
realise that health actually
varies according to the
amount of laughter.
We choose our joys and
sorrows long before we
experience them.

Kahlil Gibran

Lions at a glance

One of the biggest things I've learned is that I don't always have to be right.

Jeffrey B. Swartz, CEO, Timberland Co.

Making a Difference

A man was walking along the beach when he noticed
a figure in the distance. As he got closer, he realised
the figure was that of a boy picking something up and
gently throwing it into the ocean. Approaching the
boy, he asked him what he was doing.

"I'm throwing the starfish back into the ocean,"
the boy replied.
"The sun's up and the tide's going out.
If I don't throw them back, they'll die."

"Son," the man said, "don't you realise there are
miles and miles of beach and hundreds of starfish?
You can't possibly make a difference."

The boy listened politely. Then he bent down,
picked up another starfish and threw it into the surf.
"I made a difference for that one,"
he said with a smile.

Dominant characteristics of the lion

Task/results-oriented

Efficient and effective

Likes to be in charge

Other people may see the lion as

Wanting achievement at any cost

Forceful

Aggressive

Uncaring

Pushy

Arrogant

Closed

Self-contained

A know-all

Stubborn

Patronising

Effective

Truthful

Reliable

A high performer

Honest

Someone with integrity

A planner

Direct

How to address lions

Don't waste time.

Be brief and to the point.

Speak directly.

Spell out the bottom line.

Appointments and punctuality

Fix and keep appointments.

Punctuality matters to the lion.

If you arrive late, don't explain. Apologise and ask if the meeting is on.

To initiate a conversation with a lion

Briefly introduce the task and say what it is.

Outline the major points and the bottom line.

Don't go into detail.

Conversational structure

Main points

I speak while you listen and vice versa

3-30 seconds to make a point

How to change a lion's way of thinking and operating

Lions think their way is best. They will only accept a better way if the results can be proven.

You will need to show them why your way is better. They will find out fast if what you're saying is true. If you're wrong, you've had it.

They need to know that their opinion matters and will be counted.

They also need to know that they will get credit for what they contribute.

How to present change

Make sure the lion understands the result you want to achieve. This will show why change is necessary.

What about mistakes?

Be straight, honest and direct when telling a lion about mistakes that have been made.

Communicating negative feedback

Avoid doing this in public.

Be brief and to the point.

The lion will get over it and keep on functioning.

What do lions hate most?

Anything irrational

Incompetence

Being cheated

Dealing with detail

Having their freedom curtailed

Lateness

Broken agreements

How do lions express anger?

Lions don't explode or make a show of anger, but rather use it as a tool.

The best strategy when they are angry is to treat them softly or leave them alone.

How to acknowledge a lion

Make it short. If you make it big, they will think it's a waste of time.

Lions won't believe you if you exaggerate.

Just say, "Well done - good job. The next job is ..."

If communicating by e-mail, focus on how good the lion's work is.

Getting a lion to co-operate

Make sure that what you're asking falls within the task - a lion always puts the task first.

Don't interfere with the lion's work or meetings.

Additional issues

Don't discuss emotions: lions think these just get in the way.

Before adopting anything, lions will check thoroughly.

If you want a lion to join in, say it's a process.

Present ideas with reference to someone the lion holds in high regard, and talk about what they would have done.

Use bullet form wherever possible.

Make it clear that the lion's opinion is valued.

Dolphins at a glance

Some people come into our
lives and quickly go.
Some stay for a while,
leave footprints on our hearts
and we are never the same.

Author unknown

The Dolphins

I swam and played amongst the waves,
It was a joyous day,
When suddenly I saw a sight
That drained the joy away.

A deep dark shape beneath the surf -
My heart was filled with fear.
I was alone, defenceless,
And help was nowhere near.

Then bursting through the water
In a cloud of glistening spray,
A pod of friendly dolphins
Leapt, and they began to play

Around me in the ocean.
Their smiling faces beamed.
The deep dark shape had vanished.
Life was better than I'd dreamed.

And now when I remember
That magical perfect day
The dolphins came to play with me
Together in the bay,

I see that simply smiling,
Or reaching out a hand,
Can change the day from bad to good
And leave you feeling grand.

Sometimes the day is dreary
And life seems one huge plot
To make you feel disastrous,
And lose every joy you've got.

That's when you need a dolphin,
A friendly face, a smile.
Someone who takes an interest,
Who'll listen for a while.

Yadrif Desh

Dominant characteristics of the dolphin

Sensitive

Tuned in to peoples emotions

Vulnerable

Interested in details

Other people may see the dolphin as

Too emotional

Weak

Not serious

Not effective

Too concerned with detail

Sociable

A good friend

Loving

Supportive

Precise

Understanding

How to address dolphins

Use a quiet tone of voice.

Be gentle.

Be prepared to go into detail.

Appointments and punctuality

Dolphins prefer punctuality, but if you are late they will accept you and say nothing.

They feel more stressed than their "nice guy" appearance might suggest.

To initiate a conversation with a dolphin

Start with a greeting.

Ask meaningful questions.

Show an interest.

Listen and interact.

Conversational structure

Provide detailed explanations.

Give plenty of eye contact.

Express your emotions.

How to change a dolphin's way of thinking and operating

Ask questions.

Show how the change will improve the situation and benefit others.

Present a logical case.

How to present change

Advise in advance.

Don't impose change immediately.

Go into detail.

What about mistakes?

Talk to the dolphin privately and quietly.

Say "we" instead of "you".

Communicating negative feedback

Say "we" and "us", even if you need to fire the dolphin.

Be fair.

What do dolphins hate most?

Being shouted at

Sudden change

Negative feedback in public

Finding that people are not interested

How do dolphins express anger?

Instead of showing anger, dolphins keep it inside.

If they are angry they will probably apologise.

How to acknowledge a dolphin

Do this gently, avoiding exposure.

Flowers and notes are welcome, but don't make a big show.

If communicating by e-mail, emphasise how the dolphin impacts the team.

Getting dolphins to co-operate

Rather than telling them what to do, ask for their help.

Treat them gently.

Additional issues

Togetherness is important to dolphins.

They like material that gives them the whole picture and shows
how everyone fits in.

If they don't have the information they need, they may feel unvalued.
So keep asking them to make sure they feel involved.

Dolphins generally do not say what is going on for them.

Elephants at a glance

Let me tell you the secret that
has led me to my goal.
My strength lies solely in
my tenacity.

Louis Pasteur

If children live with criticism, they learn to condemn.

If children live with hostility, they learn to fight.

If children live with fear, they learn to be afraid.

If children live with pity, they learn to feel sorry for themselves.

If children live with ridicule, they learn to feel shy.

If children live with jealousy, they learn to feel envy.

If children live with shame, they learn to feel guilty.

If children live with encouragement, they learn to be confident.

If children live with tolerance, they learn to be patient.

If children live with praise, they learn appreciation.

If children live with acceptance, they learn to love.

If children live with approval, they learn to like themselves.

If children live with generosity, they learn to share.

If children live with honesty, they learn to be truthful.

If children live with justice, they learn to be fair.

If children live with kindness and consideration,
they learn respect.

If children live with security, they learn to have faith in
themselves and in those around them.

If children live with friendliness, they learn that
the world is a good place to live in.

Adapted from "Children Learn What They Live"
by Dorothy Law Nolte

Dominant characteristics of the elephant

Collects information

Needs accurate details

Likes to analyse things

Sensitive

Vulnerable

Other people may see the elephant as

A nuisance

Too fond of questions

Indecisive

Formal

A problem creator

Insensitive

Closed

Full of excuses

Accurate

Precise

Reliable

Sensitive

Honest

Capable

Logical

Analytical

How to address elephants

Talk quietly and gently.

Go into detail.

Appointments and punctuality

Elephants value punctuality. If you come late they may say nothing but will probably feel stressed.

How to initiate a conversation with an elephant

Start with a greeting.

Go into detail.

Don't talk for too long.

Conversational structure

Provide details, e.g. verified figures.

Be precise.

Supply background information.

How to change an elephant's way of thinking and operating

You must be logical in your approach.

Ask and show how the change will improve the situation and benefit people.

How to present change

Make a logical case for what you want.

Supply details.

What about mistakes?

Talk to the elephant honestly and quietly, behind closed doors, about any mistakes.

It's not enough to point out the error: you will need to explain how it came about.

Communicating negative feedback

This must be done in private.

After giving the feedback, outline 2 or 3 steps that the elephant can take to rectify any problems.

What do elephants hate most?

Change

Having mistakes pointed out in public

Being shouted at

How do elephants express anger?

They hardly show it. If they do, they have good logical reasons and will apologise afterwards.

Monkeys and elephants can drive each other wild to the point where the monkeys explode.

How to acknowledge an elephant

Be gentle.

Talk quietly, one-to-one, without any fuss.

Acknowledge their contribution in detail.

If doing this by e-mail, don't include any cc's.

Getting elephants to co-operate

This needs to be within the task. If you are not sticking to the plan, the elephant may become confused.

Elephants hate saying no and will only do so when pressed.

Additional issues

Elephants don't display emotion or say what they think.

When they feel hurt, they get their own back by not co-operating.

Personality traits

Lion (orange pages)	Monkey (yellow pages)
single-minded	playful
visionary	energetic
straight forward	extrovert
purposeful	lively
persevering	persuasive
Elephant (green pages)	**Dolphin** (blue pages)
cautious	caring
meticulous	nurturing
deliberate	supportive
sceptical	patient
formal	relaxed

Identifying the animals in your zoo

In order to communicate with your people effectively you have to recognise their individual communication styles. The master zoo keeper will study the animals carefully to identify each one accurately. Here's how:

	Monkey	Lion	Dolphin	Elephant
Behaviour	gets excited	likes to have own way	wants attention	asks a lot of questions
	relies on personal charm to get own way	is decisive	likes to be liked	seems indecisive
	has lots of ideas	has strong views	tries to be helpful	is logical
	likes lots of variety	knows own competence	supports others	likes research
Tends to ask	who? (the personal dominant question)	what? (the results - oriented question)	why? (the personal non-goal question)	how? (the technical analytical question)
Likes to save	effort likes to take the easy way	time likes to be efficient	relationships friendship means a lot to the Dolphin	face hates to look bad or get caught without enough data
Fears and dislikes	boring explanations, wasting time with too many facts	someone wasting their time, trying to decide for them	rejection, not being cared for	making a mistake

How to get the best from your people

	Monkey	Lion	Dolphin	Elephant
Best way to treat them	get excited with them show emotion	let them be in charge	be supportive show you care	give lots of data
Recognise that they assess themselves by	applause and feedback	results and goals achieved	friends and relationships "If they still like me I must be doing it right"	activity and keeping busy they believe results will fall into place
Make it possible for them to	get ahead quickly and face new challenges	get into competitive situations - they like to win	relax and feel good, knowing that you care	be let off the hook, not feel cornered or pressured into making a decision
Help them improve by	giving them recognition and some structure within which to reach the goal	giving them a position which requires co-operation with others	providing a structure of goals showing them methods for achieving each goal	encouraging them to develop communication skills so they can relate better to other people
Lead them effectively by	inspiring them to bigger and better accomplishments with short-term schedules	allowing them freedom to do things their own way	outlining specific plans and activities to be accomplished	giving them structure, a framework or "track" to follow
Give presentations that	include jokes and funny stories	give information quickly, and use bullet points	include heart-warming stories	include data presented logically using Powerpoint

Quick guide to the communication styles

	Monkey	Lion	Dolphin	Elephant
Need to learn	discipline, to think it through, to pause	humility, feelings, to listen to others, to follow	determination, to reach for goals, to act without agreement	initiative, to act, to enjoy, to appear wrong
Must be allowed to	get ahead quickly with a fast-moving challenge	know the score, get into competitive situations and win (or appear to)	relax and feel good about the people around them	be let off the hook, not be cornered or pressured
Take endorsement from	social skills - they like to be good at winning people over	getting the job done well and on time	friends and relationships	knowledge - they relate to others around information
Become most effective with	some direction with which to reach goals	positions of authority and responsibility	structure and methods to reach goals	avenues to apply logical analysis
Rely on the power of	charm: expect to win people over	competence: know they're strong enough to win it	acceptance: the ability to please others will save the day	expertise: when in doubt bring in more data
On the job excel at	promotion, ideas, drama, marketing, graphics, art	organisation, development, planning, management, co-ordination	service, social or relationship tasks, personnel, teaching	research and development, analysis, statistics, data gathering

Further Applications

For further information about applying this system in specific situations, such as:

- giving business presentations

- communicating with your children

- resolving conflicts at home or at work

- helping a new colleague to fit in

- promoting your business

contact Nigel Risner

Garden House
Garden Close
Arkley
Herts EN5 3EW
England

E-mail: Nigel@nigelrisner.com

Tel: +44 (0)20 8447 1732

If you would like to receive weekly updates and inspirational thoughts and suggestions from Nigel, please e-mail him today and you will be added to the list.

Other Titles by Nigel Risner

Coming in spring 2006 – The I.M.P.A.C.T Code

Discover the six principals that will allow you to live the life you have always wanted in this exciting new book with a hidden reward for anyone who breaks the code!

"You Had me at Hello" – The New Rules for Better Networking

"It's a Zoo Around Here!" – The New Rules for Better Communication

"Mastermind it" – The New Rules for Better Goal Setting

Risner's Reminders:

10 Steps to Becoming an Effective Leader

10 Steps to Becoming Personally Empowered

10 Steps to Effective Time Management

10 Steps to Getting What you Deserve

10 Steps to Reaching Your Goals

10 Traits to Highly Successful People

Audio-visual tools for self-development

Moments of Truth set of 12 audio CDs

Self Mastery for Your Personal Success video, audio (3 cassettes for 2 CDs) and workbook

To order any of these titles or to find out more information about the complete range of services available from Nigel Risner contact us on:

Tel: +44 (0) 20 8447 1732

Email: Nigel@nigelrisner.com

Nigel Risner

The only motivational speaker in Europe to
have been awarded Speaker of the Year from
both The Academy of Chief Executives and
The Executive Committee, Nigel is a
respected author, television presenter
and a prolific speaker. He speaks with
authority: his own life having veered perilously
away from comfortable norms at times. He has learned
that positive results can come from negative experiences, and that
we often learn best from situations which are unfamiliar and even uncomfortable.

As one of the youngest CEO's of a financial services company in the City of
London, Nigel knows business as well as he knows life and more importantly he
knows what it takes to lead a successful business! Unlike other speakers or
consultants, he has the ability to translate - with electrifying effect - that hands on
experience into a coherent, compelling and exciting philosophy, which has made
him one of Europe's leading speakers and a powerful professional coach to some
of the world's leading business executives.

Today he conducts more than 150 seminars and speeches a year for an enormous
variety of companies and organisations in Britain and overseas. When he isn't
travelling Nigel lives with his wife and two children in Hertfordshire.